PICTURES to PARAGRAPHS

WRITING POETRY

Leslie Holleran

Lerner Publications ◆ Minneapolis

Lerner Publications Company
An imprint of Lerner Publishing Group, Inc.
241 First Avenue North
Minneapolis, MN 55401 USA

For reading levels and more information, look up this title at www.lernerbooks.com.

Main body text set in Aptifer Sans LT Pro.
Typeface provided by Linotype AG.

Editor: Nicole Berglund **Designer:** Emily Harris **Photo Editor:** Angel Kidd
Lerner team: Martha Kranes

Library of Congress Cataloging-in-Publication Data

Names: Holleran, Leslie author
Title: Writing poetry / Leslie Holleran.
Description: Minneapolis : Lerner Publications, 2026. | Series: Pictures to paragraphs | Includes bibliographical references and index. | Audience: Ages 8–12 | Audience: Grades 4–6 | Summary: "Poetry can be a short haiku or an extended free verse. Readers use photo prompts to learn about and practice writing different kinds of poems"— Provided by publisher.
Identifiers: LCCN 2025016358 (print) | LCCN 2025016359 (ebook) | ISBN 9798765688779 library binding | ISBN 9798348028763 paperback | ISBN 9798765695821 epub
Subjects: LCSH: Poetry—Authorship—Juvenile literature
Classification: LCC PN1059.A9 H66 2026 (print) | LCC PN1059.A9 (ebook) | DDC 808.1—dc23/eng/20250404

LC record available at https://lccn.loc.gov/2025016358
LC ebook record available at https://lccn.loc.gov/2025016359

Manufactured in the United States of America
1-1012672-54707-6/18/2025

TABLE OF CONTENTS

POETRY TODAY

A poem has rhythm and flow. This is because poetry was originally spoken. That characteristic sets it apart from other kinds of writing. Poetry's oral tradition continues today with poetry readings and slams.

Poetry often expresses emotions such as happiness, sadness, love, or wonder. It can cover any subject. Poetry is written in lines. A line or set of lines creates a stanza. Poems can be long or short. All poems are concise. They use as few words as possible to communicate meaning.

Writing poetry involves three stages. In the first stage, writers plan. They think about what they are going to write and how they will write it. There are many poetic forms to choose from. Then they write a first draft.

In the second stage, writers share their poems with peers. After writers get feedback, they consider the suggestions and then revise. In the third stage, writers finish editing their poems, and then they may publish them. Let's learn more about writing poetry. Photo prompts will spark your imagination and inspire your words.

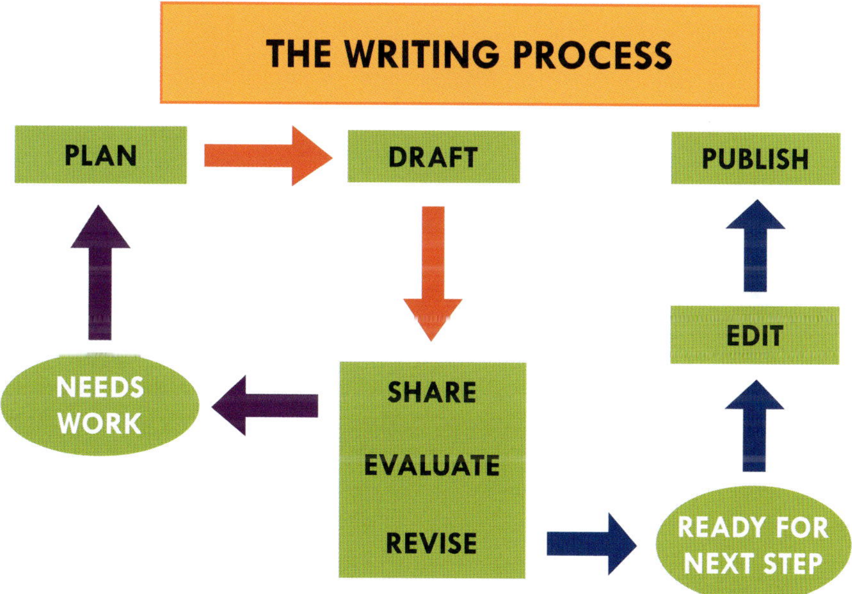

CHAPTER 1

PAINT A PICTURE WITH WORDS

Poetry creates vivid images in your mind with different techniques. To do this, it relies heavily on the senses—hearing, sight, smell, taste, and touch. Poets use literary devices including personification, metaphor, and simile to make comparisons and create imagery with words. Poets can draw on emotions and perspectives to write impactful poetry.

Poets have brought countless objects, from flowers to silverware, to life with personification. At the end of the nursery rhyme "Hey Diddle Diddle," a dish and spoon run. Over a hundred years ago, a reporter dubbed New York City "The City That Never Sleeps." That writer was using personification. You'll find examples of poetic devices in many different kinds of writing because they're so helpful in creating vivid descriptions.

The tone of a poem is the mood that it sets through its word choice. The following poem, "An Unwelcome Visitor," personifies a hurricane as someone you don't want to pass through your town. How would you describe its tone?

An Unwelcome Visitor

Skies grew dark
Day turned into night at noon

Winds as fast as race cars tore
through,
while waves pounded the shore

Rain made rivers out of streets
People sheltered out of sight

As quickly as the hurricane came,
it left
Destruction in its path

An unwelcome visitor
likely to return
again someday

WRITING PROMPT: BRING NATURE TO LIFE

Imagine that the hurricane shown in this photo is a person or group of people. Bring the great outdoors to life using personification in a poem.

Some similes you've probably heard are "busy as a bee" and "cold as ice." A simile uses the words *like* or *as* to compare things. Try not to use similes you've heard before in your writing, though. Come up with something fresh instead. Use your imagination and let your writing be as original as you are.

In a metaphor, poets compare qualities that two things share. But in contrast to similes, metaphors do not rely on *like* or *as*. So sometimes metaphors are harder to spot. Extended metaphors create a comparison over several lines. An entire poem could be an extended metaphor.

A familiar figure of speech for someone who likes to lounge a lot is *couch potato.* Here, *couch potato* is used as a metaphor, and it is the subject for a short poem.

Couch Potato

Lumpy, unmoving
She stays warm under
  the covers
Relaxing all day
She is a couch potato

WRITING PROMPT: MAKING COMPARISONS

Describe this scene of cherry blossoms in full bloom around the tidal basin in Washington, DC, using similes or metaphors. Does the scene give you a particular feeling you want to describe? Or maybe you're inspired by the shapes of the blossoms and how they remind you of spring. You could use the photo as a springboard to talk about that season.

CHAPTER 2

MAKE MUSIC

The sounds that words create are important to poetry. A poet chooses specific words both for their meaning and their sound. Poems can be pleasing to the ear. Or they can be purposefully harsh for effect.

A poem may have a specific meter. That means that each line has a rhythm. Just as you sometimes clap along to a song, you can clap out the syllables in the lines of a poem to see if it has a meter.

The rhythm of a poem's meter is similar to the beat of a drum.

The lullaby "Twinkle, Twinkle, Little Star" has both meter and rhyme. Each line has seven beats. The first and second lines, as well as the third and fourth, rhyme. Pairs of rhymes are called couplets. "Twinkle, Twinkle, Little Star" also has repetition, a very common element in poetry. Every time the word *twinkle* appears, it is said twice. Repetition helps to create rhythm.

WRITING PROMPT: RHYME

Brainstorm some pairs of words that rhyme based on this photo. Try writing some couplets. Here's an example:

Leaping tall,
Gus caught his favorite ball

Many poems today are not written in meter. When a poem doesn't have meter it's called free verse. "The Luckiest Chicken" contains rhyming couplets, but it's a free verse poem. This is a bit unusual, since free verse poems don't often rhyme. Many say there's an exception to every rule, and here's one.

The Luckiest Chicken

One day, Mae, the chicken, got lost
With that her whole world was
tossed

She decided to use her voice
She had no choice!

Cluck, cluck, cluck
She cried,
Hoping to be found

Her call was heard
She was one lucky bird

Ellie gave her a home
She no longer had to roam

Cluck, cluck, cluck . . .
She sang,
Believing she was the luckiest chicken

WRITING PROMPT: UNDER THE SURFACE

Write a free verse poem about this underwater scene. Talk about specific elements in the picture, such as the fish, rocks, or water.

CHAPTER 3
MORE SOUND EFFECTS

Onomatopoeia occurs when a word makes the sound of the action it describes. Some examples are *bang*, *bump*, *hiss*, *ring*, *splash*, *swish*, and *whack*. Sometimes these words act as nouns, or things. Sometimes they are verbs, or actions. We can describe the hooves on a trotting horse as "clacking" on the ground.

Onomatopoeia appears in "The Luckiest Chicken." Do you remember which word it was? If not, read it again. Did you find it?

When the initial consonant sounds of two or more words repeat, it's called alliteration. Alliteration is found in all kinds of writing besides poetry. You also can pepper your prose with it. Here's an example of alliteration with the letter *G*: "A Great Dane growled and chewed his bone." In this example, "Great Dane growled" creates alliteration.

A poet can also choose to repeat a vowel sound. When two or more words that appear close to one another have the same vowel sound, it's called assonance. In "An Unwelcome Visitor," the words "hurricane came" contain assonance. Both of those words have a long *A* sound.

WRITING PROMPT: ROUGH WATERS

Let's go to the beach! Describe how high winds are affecting the ocean in this photo. Brainstorm as many words as you can. Then write a poetic description that includes alliteration, assonance, or both.

Anaphora is a specific kind of repetition that creates a particular sound. With anaphora, a word or several words are repeated at the beginning of each line.

I Know

I know there's so much I don't know
I know I want to know more
I know I have so far to go, but
I know that it's okay doing my best
and learning each day

WRITING PROMPT: THE BEST SUMMER EVER

Write a poem with anaphora in which each line starts with the phrase "Come summer." Feel free to let your imagination wander and include activities that aren't pictured here. What are some of your favorite things to do in summer? Come up with as many as you can and create a poem describing the best summer ever.

CHAPTER 4

GIVE IT A GO

Acrostic, haiku, and limerick poems all have a particular structure for their verses. However, there's a great deal of room for creativity in terms of word choice. That's entirely up to you!

Limericks are humorous nonsense poems intended to make you laugh. They often tell a short, funny story about a person. Limericks have a distinctive rhyme scheme and meter. The first, second, and fifth lines rhyme with one another, and each have eight beats. Lines three and four share a different rhyme and are shorter with only five beats. Here's a limerick written to celebrate a woman's birthday.

Mary was once a caffeine queen
She liked coffee, it was so keen
She met a nice guy
They wed by and by
What a life for Mary it's been

Traditionally inspired by nature, haiku are simple, direct poems that don't rhyme. The structure is three lines with seventeen syllables total. The first line has five syllables, the second line has seven, and the third line has five. Here's an example:

Woof, woof barks Otis
Someone is at the front door
Dog is a doorbell

WRITING PROMPT: TASTY TREATS

Here's your chance to create a haiku of your own. Can you describe the colors of the gumdrops and how they taste? If you've never eaten a gumdrop, imagine how you'd want it to taste.

In acrostic poems, the subject is written vertically down the page. The first letter of each line begins a word or words describing the subject. In the example below, the subject is a person named Leslie with each word or words describing her.

Listener
Earthy
Smart
Loves to move
Intelligent
Easygoing

Using these prompts, you have written poetry. You can find inspiration in other places too. Take a walk outside and notice any plants, animals, or buildings around you. Or look around your home and think about the objects you see. Now that you have practiced your poetry and understand the writing process, you are a poet!

WRITING PROMPT: ALL ABOUT ME

Write an acrostic poem using either your name or a favorite hobby as the subject. Hobbies can be anything you enjoy doing, such as a sport, an art form, or playing an instrument.

GLOSSARY

anaphora: the repetition of a word or phrase at the beginning of a series of lines

assonance: the repetition of a vowel sound in a line or series of lines

free verse: poetry lacking meter

metaphor: a comparison between two things that have something in common

meter: a pattern of beats in a line of poetry, created by the number of syllables

onomatopoeia: a word that makes the sound of the action it describes

personification: an object or thing described as having a human trait

prose: the ordinary language people use in speaking and writing, as opposed to metrical verse used in poetry

rhyme: a similar sound, usually occurring at the end of two or more lines

simile: a comparison using the words *like* or *as*

LEARN MORE

Britannica Kids: Poetry
https://kids.britannica.com/kids/article/poetry/353645

The Children's Poetry Archive
https://childrens.poetryarchive.org

Cleary, Brian P. *Eating My Words and 128 Other Poems*. Millbrook Press, 2024.

Kiddle: Poetry Facts for Kids
https://kids.kiddle.co/Poetry

Kooser, Ted, and Connie Wanek. *Marshmallow Clouds: Two Poets at Play Among Figures of Speech*. Candlewick Press, 2022.

Poetry Foundation: Children's Poems
https://www.poetryfoundation.org/education/children

Rebman, Nick. *Writing Poetry*. Focus Readers, 2024.

Stickney, Laura. *The Art of Poetry*. Kids Core 2025.

INDEX

PHOTO ACKNOWLEDGMENTS

Image credits: SeventyFour/Getty Images, p. 4; Alan Majchrowicz/Getty Images, p. 6; Alexander Spatari/Getty Images, p. 7; Warren Faidley/Getty Images, p. 9; John Baggaley/Getty Images, p. 11; SDI Productions/Getty Images, p. 12; FG Trade/ Getty Images, p. 13; Karim Laib/500px/Getty Images, p. 14; s5iztok/Getty Images, p. 15; visualspace/Getty Images, p. 16; VitalyEdush/Getty Images, p. 17; 1001slide/ Getty Images, p. 18; Zoom Pet Photography/Getty Images, p. 19; David Clapp/ Getty Images, p. 21; andresr/Getty Images, p. 23; Tom Werner/Getty Images, p. 24; Alexander Raths/Shutterstock, p. 25; pkphotography/Getty Images, p. 27; The Good Brigade/Getty Images, p. 29. Design elements: Olex Runda/Shutterstock; Claudio Divizia/Shutterstock.

Cover: Maria Alam Sraboni/Shutterstock.